995

Elements of
Classical Ballet
Technique

Karel Shook: Elements of Classical Ballet Technique

as practiced in the school of the

Dance Theatre of Harlem

DANCE HORIZONS · NEW YORK · 1977

The front cover and title page photograph, by Martha Swope, of Ronald Perry
in Geoffrey Holder's ballet *Dougla,* is from GREAT PERFORMANCES *Dance
in America* series, made possible by the National Endowment for the Arts, the
Corporation for Public Broadcasting and Exxon Corporation.
The back cover portrait of the author is by Snowdon.
Cover and interior design by Bert Waggott.

Copyright © 1977 by Karel Shook

All rights reserved. No part of this book may be reproduced
or utilized in any form or by any means, electronic or
mechanical, including photocopying, recording or by any
information storage and retrieval system, without permission
in writing from the Publisher.

ISBN 0-87127-093-5 (Cloth); ISBN 0-87127-098-6 (Paper)

Library of Congress Catalog Card Number: 77-81992
Printed in the United States of America

Dance Horizons, 1801 East 26th Street, Brooklyn, N.Y. 11229

" . . . . . *theory alone does not suffice for the exact demonstration of the principles of dancing, and far from augmenting the number of good dancers, mediocre instruction reduces it, as everything depends upon the elementary grounding. A bad habit once acquired is almost impossible to eradicate.*"

—Carlo Blasis, 1820

To

ALVA B. GIMBEL

with gratitude

and

affection

CONTENTS

INTRODUCTION

EACH YEAR more and more public and private schools are adding
ballet courses to their curriculum, or intramural programs—on the
elementary, high school and college levels. Other organizations—
churches, recreational centers and Y's—are following suit with equal
intensity. Beyond this, privately operated dance schools are springing
up daily across the country. The urge and need to study dance has
swept the land, and, now for the first time, countless youngsters, who
would otherwise be deprived of the opportunity, find dance instruction
available to them.

Such a proliferation means that teachers have to be found to satisfy
the growing need. But who are they and where do they come from? At
certain periods of the year the mailbox of Dance Theatre of Harlem,
and, I am sure, that of every major school in the country, is stuffed with
requests for teachers. Many of the positions offered are very nicely
paid, but the job description usually asks for a creature that exists only
on the highest professional level—if there—and one who could not
accept such a post in the first place. At the shakedown, when and if
such positions are filled, it is more likely than not with inexperienced
teachers just out of college or with those who fit into the category of
the old adage: "those who can't, teach."

The mistaken idea that the elementary grades in dance instruction,
regardless of the beginner's age, can be taught with any success, in the
absence of strict supervision, by neophyte teachers or advanced students, has to be discarded immediately. These elementary levels are
the most difficult and demanding to teach: young people without
experience who teach them need constant and expert guidance. Since
so many of the schools or organizations in which they work are in
remote areas where, unfortunately, little or no dance is seen, there is
no place for them to get the aid they so desperately need. When it is
economically possible for them, the more serious of these young
teachers spend their vacations doing intensive study in New York
City or other urban areas where they can find the help they are

seeking. Many from all over the United States, and other parts of the world as well, come to Dance Theatre of Harlem for our summer courses and at various times of the year when they are free to do so. I based much of this manual on the questions they ask most consistently.

It is curious to note that the greatest body of their problems lies not so much with the technique of dance, but with a general lack of knowledge of the disciplines surrounding the process of instruction. Perhaps permissive education has ill-prepared them for the relentless and rigid demands of dance pedagogy. It is with these disciplines and the structure into which they fit that I am chiefly concerned in these pages.

—Karel Shook

Part One:

The Antecedents

❦ I ❧

The Dance Teacher

THE ART of making a dancer is one of the most painstaking occupations in the world. It demands the precision of the architect, the patience of a lace-maker, the courage and endurance of a mountain climber. And, since the finished product is subject to inevitable mortality, the work brings great exhilaration and intense heartbreak. It is a never-ending struggle with the forces of nature to reach a summit of near-perfection achieved only a few times in the most successful careers. It is, in the true meaning of the word, tantalizing, and anyone devoting himself or herself to it must have the physical and temperamental stamina to support this condition.

The teacher's gift is inborn; it can be nurtured, but it cannot be manufactured. The urge to teach is something of a compulsion which the true instructor is unable to avoid or combat. This urge inspires a hunger for new information and the necessity to communicate the resulting knowledge to others. Thorough command of a skill or craft is important, but it is not enough. For the ballet master, technical prowess is merely a point of accomplishment that rests upon a foundation of great cultural development; this, in turn, is solidly placed upon another base: tradition, which is our link to the living past. If the ballet master does not know and understand the traditions of his own art, and all the arts related to it, he will never be able to instill in the student the qualities of an expanded humanity that make for great dancing.

Too many teachers concern themselves solely with a pragmatic routine that they are convinced cannot fail provided they follow the rules. Their approach to the subject and student is impersonal and matter-of-fact—a road that leads to a dead end. The dance teacher must be involved with the total human being, because the dancer's body is an instrument which eventually has to be able to reflect all states of the psyche. This implies a student-teacher relationship that is deep and intimate. Such relationships are balanced on a point of intensity; they are continually threatened by intrinsic dangers. The emotions have to be controlled if objectivity, which is a prerequisite of good teaching and good learning, is to be preserved. The candid

3

possibility for teacher and student to face each other, nakedly and truthfully in a two-way mirror, without any attempt at deception or profiteering, is essential.

In Russia, the dancer's teacher is as severely criticized as the artist himself. The result of the teacher's work is under constant observation, and it is acclaimed or rebuked according to the quality, whether good or bad, of the dancer's performance. Of course, in Russia, after a certain point in his development, the dancer puts his fate into the hands of a master-teacher in whom he has absolute trust and with whom he has full rapport. Each artist, therefore, has his private coach as do athletes in the United States. Such is rarely the case in the West, where the teacher assumes a much more anonymous position. If this condition were rectified, we would have better teachers in general, and, consequently, many finer dancers. Certainly our most understanding artists would surpass themselves because of the challenge, inspiration and sense of security such a situation would provide.

Unfortunately, the majority of teachers, both here and abroad, do not possess the necessary faculties and are frequently reluctant to acquire them because they are teaching out of disillusionment, disappointment in a performing career, or as a questionable second choice. The usual process of becoming a teacher follows a pattern, with variations. The dancer, having gone as far as possible in his or her home town, goes to the big city to study and seek performing opportunities, doesn't find work, so returns to the home town and opens a school. Or, does get work, but becomes disillusioned and homesick, and goes back to teach. Or, does dance successfully, reaches the point of retirement and decides to teach for a livelihood. Or, worst of all, the local teacher upon retirement turns a school over to a favorite student who has never done anything professionally. Added to these are other types that have sprung up in the recent past: the young person with an impossible body for dance who decides she or he will be a teacher; the university dance major, who has started training too late for a performing career, but gets a degree to *teach* dancing.

Out of all these categories there have emerged a few productive teachers but, considering the thousands who are teaching, the percentage is so low it is deplorable. However, many have lucrative enterprises going for them. No one is concerned with the damage they may be doing along the way.

Before entering into a career as a ballet teacher one must have had the benefit of the best training and a relative amount of practical performing experience. The decision to pursue this career must have been made out of free choice and a committment to develop, nurture, and bring into flowering the talent of others. The instructor has to be totally prepared to assume the heavy responsibilities that such work will demand of him or her. The teacher is obligated to become a medium through which tradition will be transmitted and passed on to new generations.

❦ II ❧

The American Attitude

OVER THE PAST FEW YEARS, in the course of my working travels both in the United States and Europe, it has become increasingly evident to me that, while we appear to be enjoying an ideal situation, an Eden, where dance is concerned, we actually stand in danger of a great fall if some things do not change very soon. The recent ballet boom, which has taken the art out of elitist hands and made it available to the general public, represents a growth in popularity that has increased the audience for dance, particularly ballet, from about two million to well over fifteen million in a very short time; these numbers are escalating daily. One of the motivating factors behind this new surge of interest in ballet was the defection to the West of several extraordinary dancers. The widespread attention that was given their emigrations excited an eagerness to see them perform in people who had never been or, for that matter, ever thought of going to a ballet performance. A new public, such as this, brings with it perilous demands.

The first ballets that the newly initiated want to see are the nineteenth century classics—*Swan Lake, Giselle, The Nutcracker, The Sleeping Beauty, Coppélia*—all of these are works in which the émigré superstars excel because of their training and background. Each of these ballets represents a huge production, demanding a large company of dancers, a small symphony orchestra, tons of scenery and hundreds of elaborate costumes, not to mention hours of rehearsal time. All this costs enormous amounts of money. Ways to cut steadily rising costs have to be found and one of the easiest is to reduce the rehearsal time which prepares the dancers for what they must do. The result is a poorly drilled, unmotivated corps de ballet dancing behind a couple of glittering stars. Art is hardly served.

All of the enduring classic ballets have individual styles that set them apart from each other. If stylistic distinctions are not preserved, these choreographic masterpieces are reduced to something that is little more than superficial travesty. The ballabile waltz in the second act of *Swan Lake,* with its expression of the melancoly yearning of young women who have been transformed into swans and thus deprived of fulfilling the natural life for which they were born, is as important as the pas de deux that follows because it sets up a dramatic situation out of which the encounter of Odette and the Prince is a logical progression. If the women dancing this scene are not properly motivated, or do not understand what they are doing, the emotional impact that the choreographer wanted to make is dissipated—if not destroyed. These sixteen dancers must be convinced that they are each, and collectively, as prominent in what happens in *Swan Lake* as the protagonists. To achieve this, enough teachers and ballet masters must be provided who are equal to the tasks assigned them and who are given sufficient time to fulfill their responsibilities. In ballet, even though we now have some methods of notation which can record the steps, but not indicate with what style or dynamics they should be done, we are still obliged to respect tradition in its truest sense—that is, unwritten customs handed down by word of mouth or by example. In short, it would be wiser to modify the decor and improve the dancing. In theatrical dance we are now faced with the fact that a superfluity of anything encourages decadence, if the abundance is not controlled, or we lose contact with the guidelines of the living past.

Of course, the present enthusiasm for dance in the United States did not begin just a couple years ago with a small exodus of fine artists out of Russia. America has always had dance, in fact we may be the dancingest people in the world. We have had fine schools for a long time, potent teachers, splendid dancers and great companies. The enormous cultural contribution of such companies as the old Chicago Opera Ballet, the Littlefield Ballet, the San Francisco Ballet, the Ballet Russe de Monte Carlo, American Ballet Theatre, and New York City Ballet with its forerunners (The American Ballet, Ballet Caravan, Ballet Society) cannot be underestimated or overlooked.

Parellel with these we have the astonishing creativity of the modern dancers—Isadora Duncan, Ruth St. Denis, Ted Shawn, Martha Graham, Doris Humphrey, Charles Weidman, José Limón, Anna Sokolow, Helen Tamiris, Lester Horton, Valerie Bettis, Bella Lewitzky, and Katherine Dunham, all of whom sprang out of the heart of America. With them must be included Hanya Holm, who sprang out of Germany into the heart of America.

And before these men and women in time were our first classical artists among whom, to name only a few, were Mary Ann Lee (our first Giselle), Augusta Maywood, Lola Montez, Julia Turnbull, John Durang, and George Washington Smith (our first Albrecht).

It is strange that in the face of such a heritage there are still many who keep insisting that we have no American dance tradition. This is possibly because our general historians have chosen to ignore it. Out of

Calvinistic prejudice, or a fanatical dedication to distorted moral visions, they have always attempted to whitewash our founding fathers, thus obscuring the ferocious humanity of these men and women. They are quick to relate such simplistic legends as that of George Washington and the cherry tree; they don't often remind us that Washington was a fine dancer with a well-turned leg, elegant style and an eye for the ladies. Nor is much mention made of the impact of Fanny Elssler's American tour. When she first appeared in Washington, D.C., on July 11, 1840, Congress adjourned to see her, and John Quincy Adams led the applause. The House of Representatives was totally disrupted for three days and couldn't get a quorum until eleven o'clock at night because everyone was in the theater. A special reception was given for Elssler at the White House during which toasts were drunk from her slipper, and Martin van Buren presented her with a cross carved from the wood of George Washington's bier. Our historians sometimes mention great actors or actresses—Edwin Booth in *Hamlet,* or Charlotte Cushman, but they rarely record the fact that in 1846, a little over four years after its première in Paris, *Giselle* was given in Boston with two native Americans in the leading roles.

Americans have always been somewhat suspicious of tradition. Perhaps it represented Old World ways from which we were trying to escape. But, almost covertly, we have clung to it with great tenacity. It is possible that in our haste to succeed we have never really understood what it means. This is certainly true in relationship to our artistic traditions. The pioneers, crossing the plains under conditions of nearly unsurmountable hardship, carried with them heirlooms that bound them to the culture of their forebears. Grand pianos did not travel well in covered wagons, but violins presented no problem and only a fiddler, a caller, and the urge for much-needed recreation were necessary to get a square dance going, and those square dances did get going. The pioneers' isolation forced them to make their own entertainment, and dancing was one of the best ways to do it.

The square dance, whether it was done in an enclosure surrounded by covered wagons, or in a newly built barn, could trace its origins back to the dances of the sixteenth and seventeenth centuries. These dances—the Basse Danse, the Pavane, the Galliarde, the Allemande, the Bourrée, the Courante, the Gigue, the Volta—can all be compared to the vernacular dances of today. They were originated by the common people and later refined in the courts, where the steps of each dance and its patterns became the foundation upon which the art of ballet was established. What was of interest in the ballroom went onto the stage with transformations. They also remain the basis from which our presently popular social dances have sprung. It is not possible to imagine the Hustle without the Galliarde or the Waltz without the rhythmically sophisticated Volta in which the cavalier lifted his partner off the floor as she jumped. This was the dance most favored by Queen Elizabeth I.

With dance, in whatever form, we are in immediate touch with a far-reaching past. In this lies the essence of tradition—our link to that past and our means of preserving what has been of worth. This may hold more true in dance than in any other art. But tradition must be kept flowing like a swiftly moving river or it soon dams up into pockets of water that become stagnant pools. Curiously enough, in dance, it has been in what we consider traditionless America that these waters have been kept flowing in this century.

It is interesting to note that, in its time-space progression, ballet tradition, accumulating as it went along, moved northward and eastward. It traveled northward from Italy to France to Denmark and Sweden and then veered eastward to Russia. But it invaded America with French, Italians, Danes and Russians coming westward from Europe, and with Russians travelling eastward through China to America. We were destined, so to speak, to bring the art to a new renaissance. The ground has been fertile, the climate is right, but, as in wine culture, another great tradition, it takes many years for the vines to produce quality grapes. Where ballet is concerned we Americans are now into the production of vintage and champagne. In times of such superabundance we have to be especially careful to protect the vines and defy Nature, if necessary, to ensure their future. It rests with the teachers to do this. It has always been this way.

✌ III ✌

Classical Ballet

THE CLASSICAL BALLET that we practice today was invented and developed by men and women of artistic and scientific acumen over some hundreds of years. And, as long as there have been dancing academies, there have been convoluted discussions on schools, methods, systems and styles, most of them meaninglessly polemical. In this century, with an ever-increasing speed of communication and exchange of ideas among people of far-distant places, we have found that style and basic schooling are two different things; the latter remains fairly constant while the former is subject to infinite and stimulating variation. All dancers, regardless of ethnic background and whatever shading it will bring to the language their bodies speak, begin and end their careers with the same basic movements. This is to say that an *arabesque,* while remaining just what it is, will look one way on a Russian body, different on an oriental body, or on the black bodies of the dancers of Dance Theatre of Harlem. A dancer's physical proportions will determine the look of a line although the fundamental execution of any given movement has not been disturbed. What we must be concerned with is the correctness with which these actions are taught and performed.

Classical ballet, like everything else in the human condition, evolves, and, as it evolves, mutates. If it becomes static, as it has done in a few periods of history, the results are disastrous. Note the condition of French ballet, or for that matter any opera ballet, at the end of the nineteenth century and the beginning of the present. Or, observe the choreographic poverty in Russia today where socialistic ideology has repressed freedom of artistic expression with the resultant arrest of tradition's flow.

A glance at the history of ballet makes this evolutionary process clear. The germ of the theatrical convention that was soon to be called ballet first manifested itself in Italy in the form of elaborate pageants or masques produced to celebrate grand occasions. Included in these spectacles were many danced entrées. In fact, the term "ballet" and our common word "ball" are both derived from the Italian verb ballare (to dance). Royal weddings and the emigrations, usually of the bride, that attended them, brought the fledgling art to France, where it flourished in the court of Louis XIV, himself an amateur dancer with the ambitions of a professional. It might be said that ballet as we know it today began at the precise moment when the Sun King arose, stepped down from his throne, and danced. Louis recognized immediately the need to develop this new art in a logical, well disciplined way, and the first formal French academy was established in Paris in 1661 at the instigation of Cardinal Mazarin. When Louis got beyond the age to perform, ballet was banned from the court, but the Académie Royale de Danse functioned until 1780 when it was ferociously attacked by Jean-Georges Noverre for its long outdated methods and reactionary stagnation, and was forced to close its doors.

The oldest known dance academy was founded in Stockholm at the royal court in 1638 under the direction of a Frenchman, Antoine de Beaulieu, and ballet in Sweden flowered in the seventeenth and eighteenth centuries, especially during the flamboyant reign of Gustavus III, with French and Italian ballet masters and with predominantly Italian dancers. These imported artists were forced to stay for long periods of time in the north because the inclement winters prevented facile travelling. In fact, the dressing rooms in the beautifully preserved theater at the summer palace of Drottningholm were fitted out as living quarters.

In 1667, the Académie Royale de Musique, which was the official name for the Paris Opéra, was founded, and when the composer, Jean-Baptiste Lully, who had been a musician and dancer at the court of Louis XIV, took over as director in 1672 he formed a ballet school with twelve girls and twelve boys, which was the foundation of today's school of the Opéra.

In 1734, a French ballet master, Jean-Baptiste Landé, went to St. Petersburg from Sweden and with the help of Rinaldi Fossano, who had been giving dance lessons to the children of the Czar and other aristocrats, arranged a performance with these children that inspired the establishment to form a school involving the children of the Orphanage, and Russian ballet was instituted.

The Royal Danish Ballet began in 1748, again with French and Italian ballet masters and choreographers. In the mid-nineteenth century its first native choreographer of genius, August Bournonville, whose methods of teaching and whose ballets are still preserved today, brought Danish ballet to a refined splendor with a magnificent tradition.

Italy's most famous academy, the Imperiale Regia Accademia di Ballo, attached to Milan's great opera house, La Scala, did not come into being until 1821.

In 1847, a French dancer, Marius Petipa, went to St. Petersburg to perform, was widely acclaimed and stayed on to become the greatest choreographer of the nineteenth century. He was joined in 1887 by an Italian dancer and teacher, Enrico Cecchetti, who became ballet master of the Maryinsky Theater three years later and, two years after that was given the post of professor at the Imperial Academy. Cecchetti, a splendid technician, brought to the Russian school a standard of brilliance and stamina that until his time was considered beyond the dancers' limitations.

Prior to the arrival in Russia of either Petipa or Cecchetti, Christian Johansson, a product of the Royal Swedish Ballet and a student of Bournonville, had come to St. Petersburg in 1837, as a leading dancer and, after a long and distinguished career, began teaching in 1860. It was with Johansson that the true Russian technique with its light jumps, soaring leaps, swift *pirouettes* and expansive *port de bras* began to develop.

These three men—a Frenchman, a Dane and an Italian—brought the art of ballet to a flowering in Russia that was overwhelming. Together they produced Kschessinskaya, Egorova, Preobrajenska, Pavlova, Karsavina, P. Gerdt, N. Legat and Nijinsky, to name only a few. Their influence was also responsible for the development of a woman who was destined to project their pedagogy into the twentieth century—Agrippina Vaganova.

In 1909, Serge Diaghilev produced his Ballets Russes in western Europe and on the model that he presented, that is, the program format of three or four short, contrasting ballets in an evening as opposed to a full-length work, most of the companies of our time have been formed. In the United States the best known of the type were or are the Ballet Russe de Monte Carlo, American Ballet Theatre, the New York City Ballet, the Joffrey Ballet, and Dance Theatre of Harlem.

Within the last fifty years, events of singular importance have reshaped the structure of ballet with powerful strokes. In the early 1920s a moving force appeared in the person of Agrippina Vaganova, who, besides having an unusual gift as a teacher, with a discerning eye and a canny perception, also possessed the analytical mind of a scientist. One of the first tasks that she set herself was a consolidation and codification of ballet terminology—the French names given to each movement. Prior to this, the most exact terminology was that used by Enrico Cecchetti, but it was in some ways incomplete. Often, too, ballet terminology, in general, had become corrupted because so many teachers were obliged to teach in languages they did not totally command, or in which they were far from fluent. Vaganova separated all the various ballet movements into groups or families and gave each a precise name. In 1934 she published *Basic Principles of Classical Ballet,* which is undoubtedly the most valuable treatise that we have on the subject: for the first time the description in words of the entire range of the classical vocabulary was made clear and understandable. Vaganova wrote with economy, removed all superfluity, and thereby revealed the essentials.

In 1933, another event of enormous significance took place. Lincoln Kirstein brought George Balanchine to the United States to form a national academy of ballet. After some searching around for a locale, they settled in New York City, where they founded the School of American Ballet.

Balanchine, in possession of the finest Russian training and deep European roots, was immediately inspired by the strong, long-limbed Americans with their abundant vitality, speed, and musicality. Despite his formidable heritage as a direct choreographic successor to the traditions of Petipa, Balanchine turned his back on the idiom of long narrative ballets and began to compose works for this new breed of dancer. What he produced were ballets which were called, for lack of a better description, neo-classic. His signature works were involved with music, dancing and dancers; if they had any suggestion of a theme, it was merely a thread of an idea upon which these elements could be based. Needless to say, such ballets demanded an expansion of technique, especially for women, and soon dancers of his corps de ballet, and, by extension, all other corps de ballet, began to acquire a technical prowess that had until then been the sole possession of only the most virtuosic ballerinas.

It stands to reason that such a space-invading upsurge of technical achievement could not have happened without the collaboration of superior teachers. These Balanchine and Kirstein provided and soon the School of American Ballet had perhaps the most impressive faculty in the world, made up, as it was, of dancer-pedagogues such as Anatol Oboukoff and Pierre Vladimiroff, both of whom had been Balanchine's teachers; Muriel Stuart, a protegée of Anna Pavlova, was also on the early staff. These were later joined by Felia Doubrovska, Alexandra Danilova, Elise Reiman, Hélène Dudin, Antonina Tumkovsky and the Danish dancer, Stanley Williams. With George Balanchine in the lead, true twentieth-century ballet was established and, more specifically, American classical ballet.

But these instructors at the School of American Ballet were not alone. Concurrently, other teachers of exceptional ability were instructing privately, or in well established schools across the country. They came from different backgrounds and a diversity of schools— French, Italian and Russian. What they had in common was an unbroken link with the traditions of the past and an unswerving dedication to the art they served. Beyond this, all were superior teachers, and most had enjoyed successful dancing careers; in them, the skills of the master technician were combined with outstanding artistic sensibility. They were concerned, above all, with the language of dance and the eloquence with which its vocabulary, and the syntax which evolves from it, can be used.

A few with whom I have had personal contact and/or the privilege of their tutelage were: Edward Caton, Alexandra Fedorova, Cia Fornaroli-Toscanini, Anatol Vilzak, Vecheslav Swoboda, Igor Schwetzoff, Elisabeth Anderson-Ivantzova and Jean Yazvinsky in New York City; Laurent Novikoff, Bentley Stone and Walter Camryn, in Chicago; Carmelita Maracci, Bronislava Nijinska and Ernest Belcher, in Los Angeles; Dorothy Fisher, Lee Foley and Mary Ann Wells, in Seattle; June Roper, in Vancouver, Canada; Doris Jones, Claire Hayward and Mary Day, in Washington, D.C.; Catherine and Dorothie Littlefield, in Philadelphia; E. Virginia Williams, in Boston. These are the men and women who produced most of the leading American performing artists of the past four decades, and choreographers and company directors as well.

Many of these teachers/mentors are still teaching; those of us who were fortunate enough to study with them are teaching; and now some of our students are teaching. Ballet, as it has been since its inception, is being passed physically, from one human being to another in an endless chain of artistic communication.

In 1969, another phenomenon of American ballet sprang up: Arthur Mitchell founded the Dance Theatre of Harlem which was destined to add a new dimension to the world of theatrical dance. Needless to say, the arrival of a black classical company stirred up controversies; these, and the approbation and opposition they represented, came from both blacks and whites, each of whom seemed to be striving desperately to preserve, untouched, things that they felt to be exclusively their own. The questions arose: Why a black ballet company? Why blacks in ballet in the first place? How can the black man develop an empathy for something so contradictory to his heritage? In our time, how is it possible, in the midst of a struggle toward racial integration, to form an unintegrated dance company? At a cursory glance it is evident that both sides were equally misguided by an intensity of feeling and lack of genuine historical knowledge. This resulted in blindness and fostered prejudice.

In all human endeavor, any move toward evolution or change always breeds contention with its attendant conflicts. But this is a constructive chain of events that stimulates and challenges man to further evolution. The dramatic rise of the formerly invisible dancers, the emergence of the black as a classical dance artist, was not likely to be an exception to this rule.

Man started to dance the moment he stood up on two feet; no one knows what color he was then. It didn't matter, as it doesn't matter now. It took us a long time to learn to discriminate among colors, races and creeds. Primal man had no prejudices, nor does any baby born today. Prejudices are sophisticatedly acquired tastes that destroy innocence, that state of purity in which man can be in accord with himself, his fellow men, and attuned to nature. This innocence is one of the intrinsic beauties of man and if we do not regain it soon, we will perish. True dance, in any of its myriad forms, is an expression of this innocence and it is through dance that man has the possibility to find himself again. Skin shades and ethnic backgrounds have little or nothing to do with it.

It has been said that the history of man can be read in how he danced. In dance, the psyche is distilled to essence. On the dance floor, be it the pounded earth of a tribal village, the polished parquet of a ballroom, or the worn boards of a stage, all boundaries are loosened or dissolved and man is free to re-create exactly what he is—without dissimulation of any kind. In dance man assuages the spirits, whether good or evil; he cleanses his soul and revivifies his body; he prepares for war; he honors his partner and he entertains his companions. He experiences love; he epitomizes "soul." And above all—he plays. Without play, genuine play, man deteriorates into a functionary being. Beyond the basics of food, shelter, and clothing, man has other fundamental needs—faith in something or someone greater than himself; sexual expression and satisfaction, and the need to play. The *homo-sapiens* is also the *homo-ludens,* a human aspect that cannot be overlooked.

Man dances for and with his gods and therefore becomes one with them. David danced before the Ark of the Covenant to express his deepest feelings for the Jehovah he revered. The ecstatic possessions of Shango or Macumba dancers are contemporary reflections of the fervor David experienced.

The ritual that is dance in its primitive expressions must extend itself even to the reaches of the most complex theatrical dance. If it does not, if the spirit of ritual is lost, dance, however marvelously produced or performed, degenerates into a parading convention that is painfully shallow and the worst kind of hedonism. It becomes a form of self-indulgence that is intolerable.

Good dancers understand this ritual instinctively and maintain it even in the purest of classical ballets. They let their love, their exultation pour across the footlights from the space of the stage to the space of the auditorium. This active projection engages the spectator and pulls him into the dancers' circle with a response that is emotional as well as kinesthetic. The entire space is enlivened and the viewer becomes an active participant in the rite, as opposed to an isolated spectator. The result is a vital experience that is often dismaying to those who prefer prettiness to beauty or sentimentality to true feeling. Many find that, face to face with this kind of dancing, they have to learn to look at ballet in a new way, and open themselves to the total involvement demanded. Once this has been experienced, ethnic barriers will be broken down and it will be much easier to understand how and why diverse elements of different heritages and cultures can find a natural place in the serene realm of the *arabesque* and the *entrechat*. Black dancers have been practicing this for a long time and the Dance Theatre of Harlem, with its freedom of expression and firm classicism, has made it manifest.

~IV~

Dance Theatre of Harlem

TO UNDERSTAND THE SIGNIFICANCE of Dance Theatre of Harlem one must be able to observe it in historical and societal perspective. This is difficult because, although recently a great deal has been talked about black dance, very little has been properly recorded. To try to reduce the history of black dance to a paragraph is as futile as attempting to make a synopsis of the Bible. Its ancient and infinite riches penetrate so deeply into the remotest past the sources have been obscured. It is the Watusis and Masais, the Cakewalk, the Turkey Trot, the Strut, the Minuet, the Black Bottom, the Shango, the Belé, the Hustle, the Monkey and a Dance Theatre of Harlem performance of George Balanchine's *Agon*. It is Africa and Afro-America, in all their manifestations of cultures and sub-cultures. It is the West Indies, the Caribbean and all the Americas. Aside from the dances of the American Indians, we have only one indigenous American dance—the tap dance, which was developed (from clog dancing) and enriched by blacks. When it comes to what many consider the audaciousness of blacks entering one of the last strongholds of Caucasian culture, namely the classical ballet, we see that this step was a perfectly natural one; only the right time had to be awaited before it could be taken.

In the 1930s one of America's finest dancers, Sono Osato, was a curiosity because she was Japanese. The recent revelation that China has highly developed ballet dancers and companies was a surprise to many people. We must also observe the classical companies in Egypt, Iran, Turkey, Japan, Cuba, the Philippines, Mexico and Hawaii. Classical ballet has always been unethnic, employing a language that is universally understood. If we consider that this language has been developing for four hundred years and that the black dancer has been practicing it for less than fifty years, that there are still many schools in the United States that will not admit black youngsters to the classic discipline, the miracle of the emergence of Dance Theatre of Harlem is a testament to the expansive richness of the art and the tenacity of artists who happen to be black.

It has been argued that Dance Theatre of Harlem is not the first black classical company, nor its dancers the first black classical dancers. Dance Theatre of Harlem has never made these claims, but it is the first *permanently* established black company—something it could not have become had not a great deal gone before to prepare the way.

It is rumored that George Washington Smith, one of the first American premier danseurs, who partnered Fanny Elssler on her American tour, was a mulatto. We know that he started out as a clog dancer. In the last century, Juba, the black tap dancer, was proclaimed the "Greatest Dancer in the World" both here and abroad. Juba is reported to have been able to produce over one hundred and fifty different combinations of sound, which certainly brought tap dancing near to a high art form.

Homage must be paid, too, to an artist and humanitarian who was one of the "mothers of us all"—Josephine Baker. She was not a ballerina, per se, but she was an "assoluta" among the "primas." If she had not had the courage to get out of St. Louis and take her refined jazz dancing, innate elegance, taste, sassiness, and persuasive charm to Paris, which was then the art capital of the world, and make it there with the greatest of this century's geniuses, we might all, both black and white, still be floundering in semi-darkness where our art, entertainment, and enlightenment is concerned.

In the twenties of this century, Edna Guy became a protegée of Ruth St. Denis, who taught her privately, because the young black woman could not be allowed in an open class of white students. Guy, along with her partner Hemsley Winfield, gave dance recitals with great success as Hemsley Winfield's Negro Art Theatre Dance Group. What they did, of course, was what was then known as "interpretive dance," an off-shoot of the styles of Isadora Duncan and St. Denis. They were what can be called the first black modern dancers.

In the 1930s Baron Eugene von Grona, a refugee from Hitler's Third Reich, established in New York City the American Negro Ballet, a thirty-member troupe that made its debut at the Lafayette Theatre in the heart of Harlem in November of 1937. However, a study of programs and reviews reveals the fact that von Grona's use of the term "ballet" implied a certain theatrical convention rather than the traditional classic style. He was impressed with and inspired by the vigor and spontaneity of the black dancer and by jazz. It seems evident that he used these elements extremely well and his group deserved a better fate than it had. Despite the auspicious debut before an affluent white audience, von Grona could not get funds, ended up in enormous debt, and his company was disbanded.

In Chicago, circa 1930, Mark Turbyfill, a distinguished poet and ballet teacher, was determined to develop an all black classical ballet company—an urgent desire which he was never to see fulfilled. His foremost protegée was a young woman named Katherine Dunham in whom he envisioned the first black ballerina. In the early summer of 1933 Ruth Page choreographed a ballet called *La Guiablesse (The She-Devil)* based on the story of Lafcadio Hearn and with music by William Grant Still, the foremost black composer of the time. A company of fifty black dancers was recruited from all over the city of Chicago. Page, herself, danced the primary role of the She-Devil at the first performance which took place at the Century of Progress Exposition on June 16, 1933, but immediately turned it over to Dunham, who danced it at the Chicago Opera House on the 23rd of the same month. Page, in the face of Turbyfill's desire to make Dunham a classic dancer, encouraged her to devote her studies to the Afro-Caribbean styles.

When Ballet Theatre was founded in 1940 it had an adjunct group of sixteen young black women for whom Agnes de Mille choreographed a highly successful ballet, *Black Ritual*, which was based on voodoo rites of Trinidad, but at the end of the first season, the work — de Mille's first major choreographic essay — was dropped from the repertory, and the group dismissed.

In 1949, Joseph Rickhard established a company called The First Negro Classical Ballet in Los Angeles. One of the longer-lasting groups, it toured the western part of the United States until it was merged with the New York Negro Ballet which was directed by Edward Fleming and Theo Hancock, to become Ballet Americana. The company had some very strong dancers, several of whom went on to make distinguished careers. Among them were Delores Brown, Sylvester Campbell, Georgia Collins, Thelma Hill, Bernard Johnson, Charles Neal, Cleo Quitmen, Gene Sagan, Elizabeth Thompson, Barbara Wright, and Fleming, himself. The repertory, which was small, included a classic ballet, *Waltz*, with music by Lecocq, and *Folk Impressions*, based on spirituals. Both of these were choreographed by Louis Johnson and were among his first works. Ernest Parham contributed *Mardi Gras*, a clever melange of ethnic, modern and jazz styles. The only piece presented from the classical repertory was the *Blue Bird* pas de deux which was danced by Delores Brown and Bernard Johnson. The company had strong financial support from Lucy Thorndike and, after a somewhat premature New York City opening, went to England and Scotland where it was successful with both audiences and critics. While it was in England, however, Mrs. Thorndike died and the company had to be disbanded for lack of funds.

In the early 1950s Aubrey Hitchens formed the all-male Negro

Dance Theatre which, because of its basic premise, was doomed. Again, there were fine and well trained dancers—Anthony Bassae, Moore Carson, Norman Dejois, Frank Glass, Harold Gordon, Nat Horne, Bernard Johnson, James MacMillan, Charles Moore, Joe Nash, and Charles Queenan. The repertory comprised two classical works by Hitchens, Bach's *Italian Concerto* and Liszt's *Preludes,* plus two jazz-based pieces—*Outlook for Three* by Dania Krupska and *Gotham Suite* by Tony Charmoli. Ted Shawn acclaimed the company as ''an evolution in Negro dance'' but it could not survive because ballet without women is both sterile and unthinkable. Added to this, it had no funding.

In the fall of 1951 Janet Collins, until that time a unique and charming recitalist, who combined the elements of both modern and ballet in her choreography, became the prima ballerina of the Metropolitan Opera, a position that she held for several years. In the Dance of the Hours from Ponchielli's *La Gioconda* she was perhaps the first black woman that most people had seen dance on pointe. Her successor at the Metropolitan was none less than Carmen de Lavallade.

Throughout the fifties the most stable company was Katherine Dunham's; it toured endlessly and with remarkable success throughout the United States and on the Continent. Dunham insisted that her dancers study ballet and, although her wonderful theater-dance pieces, which were splendid translations to the stage of Caribbean and African dances, were not classical ballets, most of her dancers — Frances Taylor, Lenwood Morris, Leu Camacho, Tommy Gomez, Julie Robinson, and Archie Savage—moved in a balletic way, with stretched feet, long, extended line, and carried themselves with the elegance and bearing that sets the classical dancer apart. With works like *Choros* and *La Valse,* Dunham was the first black choreographer to use her dancers balletically.

In 1961, at the request of Gian Carlo Menotti, Arthur Mitchell helped to organize an integrated company to perform in the Festival of Two Worlds in Spoleto. It was called New American Ballets and was received with thunderous success. The dancers were: Pina Baush, Mary Hinkson, Akiko Kanda, Ralph Linn, William Louther, Donald McKayle, Arthur Mitchell, Robert Powell, Mabel Robinson, Kathleen Stanford, Paul Taylor, Dan Wagoner, and Dudley Williams. The program was made up of two European premières: *Meridian,* choreographed by Paul Taylor, with music by Morton Feldman, and *Games,* by Donald McKayle, with traditional music arranged by McKayle. The world premières were: *Entrance,* choreographed by Karel Shook, with music by von Reznicek; *Rainbow Round My Shoulder,* choreographed by McKayle, with a score by Robert

Cormier and Milt Okun. The final work on the program was *Toccata for Percussion,* choreographed by Herbert Ross to the music of Carlos Chavez.

Then there were individual artists who made international careers. Billy Wilson, who began his studies in Philadelphia under Sidney King and Antony Tudor, went on to become one of the leading soloists of the Dutch National Ballet, where he danced leading male roles in both classical and modern ballets. Wilson, a strong technician in all styles, had a perfectly proportioned body and a sinuousness of movement that lent elegant lyricism to everything he did. Serge Lifar created his *Maure de Venise* especially for Wilson. John Jones, another Philadelphian, and a student of Marian Cujet, was an original member of Jerome Robbins' Ballets: U.S.A. and has performed with several major companies. Jones, stark, with the attenuated body of a Giacometti sculpture, is at home in a variety of styles. Sylvester Campbell, here, in Europe, and in Canada, has done all the big classic roles—Albrecht in *Giselle,* Siegfried in *Swan Lake,* the *Corsaire,* and *Don Quixote* pas de deux, among others. He partnered Sandra Fortune in the Varna competitions on two occasions, with marked success. Campbell is basically a classic dancer with clean line, splendid elevation and fine turns. He has a cool elegance and an interior detachment that lends a special color to the roles he dances. Raven Wilkinson was a member of the Ballet Russe de Monte Carlo and the Dutch National Ballet. Betty Nichols was in the corps de ballet of Ballet Society. Talley Beatty, Louis Johnson, Arthur Bell, and Mary Hinkson, one of Martha Graham's principal soloists, have all been guest artists with Ballet Society or the New York City Ballet.

In 1954 Arthur Mitchell became a permanent member of the New York City Ballet and was soon ranked among the soloists. During his fifteen years with that company a number of important roles were created on him: among them were the pas de deux in *Agon,* Puck in *A Midsummer Night's Dream,* and the male lead in *Slaughter on Tenth Avenue.* Mitchell's handsomeness, his versatility, musicality and boundless energy, coupled with the rare ability to become whatever role he was dancing, not only put him in a class by itself, but enabled him to fit perfectly into what could have been alien territory.

Then there were others who did not perform as ballet dancers per se, but who had classical technique and the elegance and carriage that go with it. Among them were Cristyne Lawson, Carmen de Lavallade, Audrey Mason, Pearl Reynolds, Jamie Bower, Walter Nicks, Matt Turney, Ronald Frazier, Dudley Williams, Donald McKayle, Alvin Ailey, Chita Rivera, Claude Thompson, Bayork Lee, Jackie Walcott, Jaime Rogers, and Tommy Johnson. But despite the uniqueness and superiority of all the talent just mentioned, black dancers, where ballet was concerned, still occupied only one percent of the space. It took the advent of the Dance Theatre of Harlem in 1969 to consolidate black ballet and bring it in full force across the threshold of classicism.

In less than seven years Dance Theatre of Harlem grew from a modest performing group to a major force of international caliber. One of the prime reasons for the speed of this development is the fact that it was, from its inception, firmly based on a school with high standards and an effective way of teaching. On top of this, the company began performing at once and the dancers were obliged to solve any technical problems they had as swiftly as possible.

Many have called this rapid progress a miracle and, perhaps, Dance Theatre of Harlem has somehow proven that miracles do still exist, provided the will for them exists and a determination to make them happen is present in the originators of such phenomena. Miracles are, after all, quite simply the result of strongly motivated urges for achievement.

The so-called miracle of Dance Theatre of Harlem sprang directly from the human need for civil and artistic justice. The secret of the company's spectacular rise, if it is a secret, lies in the dancers themselves; the care given them by their teachers; and in the broad and varied repertory they dance—which demands of them a versatility that until now was the property of only a few special artists. The miracle springs from total dedication, and an unshakeable belief in what is being done and to what purpose, and adherence to tradition. The joie de vivre, the élan, the expansive freedom of Dance Theatre of Harlem, both company and school, is structured within the framework of a fierce discipline—that of classical ballet.

Part Two:

The Theory

✄ I ✄

Beyond Teaching

THE FOLLOWING MANUAL lays out the system of instruction in the basic principles of classical ballet that is used in the training of children and, in fact, all beginners at the Dance Theatre of Harlem. The system has been tested over several years and has proven itself both practicable and successful.

It must be understood that a manual of this type serves merely as an outline; a radiographic picture, so to speak, of a structure that is stripped of flesh and spirit. It is a point from which to move and not an end in itself.

These technical sections provide a syllabus—a definition and clarification of a method. In the teaching of classical ballet, syllabi furnish suggestions for the instructor and are reminders of the scientific approach that has to be diligently maintained. A syllabus defines a foundation—it does not impose a routine. It establishes the fact that a well constructed road exists, but only suggests a landscape. In short, while examining the skeleton we should never lose sight of the fact that we are dealing with human beings.

If necessary, this manual should be used in conjunction with Agrippina Vaganova's *Basic Principles of Classical Ballet*. In this treatise Vaganova has covered every facet of ballet instruction and each movement is clearly explained in understandable language. Another enlightening source of reference is Muriel Stuart's excellent book *The Classic Ballet*. With such studies at our disposal it would be redundant to repeat the same material here, therefore I make few attempts to describe in detail the actions that produce any given ballet movement. However, it must not be assumed that anyone can start teaching ballet from scratch with the help of books, no matter how explicit they may be. I take it for granted that those using this manual have had enough training and experience to have earned the right to teach.

Vaganova has written: "The study of any pas in classical dance is approached gradually from its rough, schematic form to expressive dance." In the early grades we concern ourselves with these "rough, schematic forms" and proceed to polish them over the six or seven years that it will take to arrive at the finished dance.

Before entering into the technical aspects of teaching it is necessary to study important points which lie beyond the teaching process, but are intimately connected to it. These points provide some of the most disputed arguments in the profession and are the source of the widest disparity of opinion.

One of the most salient questions is: "At what age should a child begin the study of classical ballet, or that of any other highly developed dance technique?" Ideally, the child should start between the ages of eight and twelve. There are few permissable exceptions to this rule. Upon entering the study of ballet the youngster should be prepared to encounter both science and art. At eight the child has had two years of academic schooling and, it is to be hoped, has acquired some basic learning skills.

Everywhere we find what are called pre-dance or pre-ballet classes for children from three to six years of age. On the surface such courses appear harmless and even beneficial, but around them lurk dangers that can grow into big problems. In the first place these classes must be in the hands of specially educated and highly specialized teachers. This rarely happens because there are so few such teachers around. The usual, and unforgivable, practice is to give over pre-dance instruction to young teachers with relatively little experience or, worse than that, to a student with no practical experience at all. Anyone undertaking the tutelage of classes at this level has to have a thorough knowledge of the functioning of the bodies and minds that are developing, but are as yet undeveloped. A complete and acute awareness of the changes these children are going through, coupled with the ability to reach them and handle them sensitively is imperative. Any attempt to teach a formal technique to children of these ages or allowing them to perform dances that put excess strain on the muscles without some technique, is taboo. Physically, unless great care is taken, the muscles of the thighs and buttocks can be swiftly overdeveloped, a condition which later may take years to correct, if it can be corrected at all.

Then there is the question of what to do with these children for the two years between the ages of six and eight when they are ready to enter into serious study. But probably the biggest problem is that, if children start too young, by the time they reach twelve or thirteen, and should be in the heart of their studies, they become bored and drop out. A few may return to dance later, but the results are usually most unsuccessful. Vital time has been lost and cannot be regained.

At the age of three the child begins to pull away from babyhood in an arc of transition that culminates in the seventh year. In this crucial seventh year the child is torn between the longing to remain a baby and the urge to step into childhood. Great attention must be paid during this period to avoid psychological or emotional dislocations which can persist for the remainder of the individual's life. The child who has not heard *Die Walküre* or had no dance lessons before the age of eight will not be culturally deprived. Little children should be taught music in some form and learn how to swim.

We often hear the phrase "she is taking ballet lessons," but rarely "she is studying ballet." At first glance there doesn't seem to be much difference between the two, but a closer look reveals the implications. The former suggests a temporary situation; the latter a long-term plan with a sense of permanency. Few parents realize, when they enroll a child in a ballet school, that they are engaging the youngster in a course of study which will cover a number of years. They also often do not understand the system of progression from one level to another. Which brings us to the question of how long ballet training takes.

Ideally, the ballet student should master the entire range of basic technique in three years of study, with two one-hour lessons weekly in the first two years and three one-hour-and-a-half lessons weekly in the third year. However, not all children will be able to accomplish this, so it is better to think in terms of three periods which will cover five years. If a class manages to cover the material laid out for the first period in nine months it is on schedule and can be progressed. If the opposite is the case the period has to be extended from three to six months. But if it takes the student any longer than that, the outlook for the future is dismal and future study should be discouraged.

When the child approaches or enters puberty, which is generally in the third or fourth year of study, provided the youngster has started at the age of eight, the teacher is faced with new challenges and must be prepared to meet them. Many teachers function perfectly in the elementary grades but cannot get beyond them with any degree of success. At this point, unless the student is transferred to a teacher who can handle the ever-increasing complications of the intermediate grades, it stands to reason that the student will not progress and will eventually drop out through boredom or discouragement.

According to my observations, with the approach of puberty, problems arise that have to be handled with care and understanding. Contrary to common belief, girls are very strong until they begin to menstruate, at which point, many begin to pass through a season of fragility which may persist until they are sixteen or even older. During this period of dramatic physical changes, some women have a tendency to blow up or put on weight. Proper nutrition is of paramount importance and severe diets must be avoided at all costs, despite the dancer's desire to be as thin as possible, or damage can be done that will never be fully repaired. Dancers who have such problems must be encouraged to put themselves on a regime which they will maintain, perhaps throughout their careers. With careful and sensible eating habits they may lose weight slowly, but the result will be a lasting one.

Boys, on the other hand, are fragile until they enter puberty, at which point their strength and resistance begin to increase. Young boys have to be made—pushed, sometimes—to work to their capacity, but all strenuous exercises have to be carefully supervised, or there is danger of the student developing hernia. Big steps such as *grand jeté entrelacé* or *grand fouetté relevé* or *sauté* cannot be introduced until the teacher is certain that the abdominal muscles are strong and controlled. Provided he has started at nine or ten years of age, a boy at fourteen should be into advanced-intermediate work and by sixteen have at his command all or most of the pyrotechnical male technique.

In general, men are slower than women, physically, because they are heavier with thicker muscles; mentally, because they lack the speed of the woman's intuitive reflexes. Moreover, the male body, except in rare cases, is tighter than that of the female, especially in the pelvic construction and, therefore, is deficient in the plastic freedom that ballet demands. Needless to say, for these and other reasons it is more difficult to make a first-class male dancer than it is to produce a ballerina. Another factor that contributes to this is that boys usually start their studies much later than girls. They often have to combat the disapproval of parents who are concerned about their boy's entering into a profession that has, until recently, carried a sexual stigma or is economically insecure. This means they are unable to begin studying until they are old enough to make and act on decisions for themselves. By this time their bodies may have matured to a degree that precludes the possibility of a career in dance.

The dilemma of how to get boys into the ballet class in the first place is overshadowed by the question of what to do with them once they get there. All teachers are eager to have boys in their schools, but too few have any knowledge of how to handle them. Many are dismayed by the common, but erroneous, belief that boys are more difficult to discipline than girls, and assume a position of offense that alienates the youngster from the beginning. In this way the cause is lost.

It is important that the boy be in the ballet school because he wants to be, and not because somebody else wishes it. There are many boys who desire to study dance, and the number is increasing steadily, but all too often the environment into which they must step to do this is uninviting. It is not easy for a pubescent boy to feel at home in a class made up exclusively of girls practicing something which, to all intents and purposes, appears to be restrictedly female. However, it is not terribly difficult to convince him why and how he has a rightful place there. Whenever it is at all possible a special boys' class should be formed. This not only eliminates self-consciousness, it also attracts other boys.

Boys have to be convinced of the basic athleticism of ballet but this must be done in a truthful way without resorting to subterfuges that are false or misleading. To tell a boy that studying ballet is going to make him a great football player is a form of deception and seduction that he will recognize, and his respect will be destroyed. There are some teachers who have boys jumping over sticks, running five laps around the studio, or pretending they are playing basketball. This is an outrageous practice for more reasons than appear on the surface. In the first place they are studying ballet, which is undoubtedly the most highly developed form of athletics that we have. It is a sport—albeit non-competitive—in itself and does not have to be equated with any other sport to gain creditability or justification. Furthermore, the comparison approach has deeper, subtler, and more insidious connotations. It implies something suspect in the fact that a man would rather dance than play football which, in turn, implies that the masculinity of a football player who likes to dance is questionable. This is denigrating to both the dancer and the sportsman because they are each operating in areas of human expression which, at the primary level, are beyond the boundaries of sexuality.

If the ballet teacher feels that his young male students need basketball or football, he should take them onto a proper court, or into a field, and coach them—if he is capable of doing so. In the ballet studio he should restrict himself to teaching them ballet, after he has adjusted his thinking about the questionability of a male doing it in the first place. If he has any doubts about his own ability to function as a male role-model he should abandon any attempt to teach youngsters of his own sex.

The ignorant assumption that all men who take pride in their bodies, and display such pride, are sexually maladjusted, is fortunately slowly being eradicated by the advancement of sexual awareness in our society.

The sexual proclivites of any human being are private and individual. It is ridiculous to categorize people sexually according to the profession they choose to follow. The fact that this has been, and continues to be done, is vital evidence that our society still has a way to go.

Dance, in all its forms, is intrinsically erotic, a condition which cannot be avoided, because the eroticism is built in. Both men and women, in a state of near nudity, and in intimate proximity to each other, do the same kind of movements in a defined space. The division between their identities, as male or female, is often obscured, but never obliterated. Indeed, devoid of the contrasts of male and female, yin and yang, dance becomes impotent, devoid of meaning, and insupportable as a humanistic demonstration or an art.

Perhaps the subject that provokes the most heated arguments is the question of when a girl should start doing *pointe* work. The answer is, quite simply, toward the middle of the third period of study. This is at the age of ten or eleven, and provided her feet and legs are strong and the muscles of the abdomen and back are sufficiently developed. Toe dancing has long been a kind of status symbol—albeit a hideous one. Some mothers, over-zealous and possibly frustrated, may want to see their little girls in tutus and toe shoes because, undoubtedly, this represents an ultimate in female achievement. These mothers are supported by teachers with one eye on the cash register, who are in turn upheld by shoe manufacturers with two eyes on the register. The dealing in toe slippers is a very lucrative business and of great advantage to all except the innocent victim—that is, the little girl. Unless the muscles are ready to support the extra stress put upon them when the dancer rises to the full *pointe,* the feet can be seriously deformed but, worse than that, the internal organs, especially those of the reproductory system, can be displaced, resulting in chronic afflictions. Unfortunately, if a scrupulous teacher refuses to put the girl on *pointe* until the right time, nine times out of ten the parent will remove her to another school which will give satisfaction.

Another issue is that of late starters—those beginning to study in the mid- or late teens. Many of our best dancers started late. Everything depends upon the condition of the muscles, the pliability of the tendons, and the willingness to work with maximum intensity. If the legs are short in proportion to the torso, if the feet are stiff with no semblance of an arch, if the back is inflexible, study should be discouraged.

In the elementary years we must always keep in mind what will be demanded of the student in the future. The training of a dancer is one long, unbroken chain of action in which each link has to be of equal strength. The eventual power of the chain is forged in the early years during which we must be exceedingly careful to test and, if necessary, strengthen any link that threatens to be weak.

↜ II ↝

Rudimentary Behavior

THE FIRST DISCIPLINES that ballet students learn are concerned with social behavior. At first glance these rules may seem arbitrary or undemocratic, but such is not the case. Adherence to certain behavior patterns instills in the student self-esteem, courtesy, and an awareness of both self and others. These qualities are carried over into the private lives of the students, who will function better as people because they have achieved self-control.

DRESS

Athletic uniforms are designed to make it easier for the athlete to play whatever game he or she plays. The same holds true for the dancer's practice clothing, which enables teachers to see, clearly, the students' bodies in action.

At Dance Theatre of Harlem girls are required to wear pink or suntan tights, chosen according to the pigmentation of their skin, and a leotard in the color designated for their particular level or class. Their ballet shoes match the color of the tights. Hair must be arranged close to the scalp or tied back neatly. No jewelry is allowed except for small earrings, if the ears are pierced. This rule can be the cause of dissension because many girls wear jewelry that has religious or superstitious significance. But it should be enforced, because necklaces and bracelets, for example, are potentially dangerous both to the wearer and those around her.

Boys are required to wear black tights, white T-shirts, short white socks and white ballet shoes.

No leg-warmers or extra wrappings are permitted for either girls or boys at any time. Neatness and cleanliness are insisted upon. Tights and leotards must be well fitted and free of wrinkles or bagginess. Perfectly fitted shoes are essential. Ballet shoes must fit snugly to support the foot without being so tight that the toes are cramped. Parents, with an understandable eye on economy, are inclined to buy shoes that are too big so that the child won't grow out of them in a few weeks. This is a very bad practice because ill-fitting shoes can inhibit the child's progress and shoes that are too big will allow the feet to spread in an undesirable way. The fact that shoes are expensive is one that must be faced.

At DTH all students have their names either printed or embroidered on the leotard or T-shirt. In smaller schools this is not necessary, but in large schools it is imperative to enable the teacher to learn the students' names.

Some teachers prefer that new beginners do not wear tights, so that they can better observe the action of the leg muscles. This is fine as long as the class dress is kept uniform. However, another snag can be hit here because, again for reasons of religion or modesty, some children are not allowed to go barelegged.

Teachers have to set the example in the question of dress. They should always wear practice or working clothes, and under no condition teach in street attire.

GENERAL CONDUCT

a) Students must enter and leave the dance studio in a quiet and orderly manner and maintain this behavior in the corridors and dressing rooms.

b) The teacher should make it clear from the first lesson that students are expected to be on time. In the question of promptness the teacher is obliged to set the example. An assistant should be provided to start the class on time in the event that the teacher is detained elsewhere. If an assistant is not available the students, regardless of age, should know how to begin the class and what to do until the teacher arrives. Any student more than ten minutes late should be asked to sit and observe the remainder of the lesson. This is not a penalty, it is a safeguard. The exercises given in the first ten minutes prepare the student's body for the rest of the class; it is inviting physical injury to allow anyone to enter too late.

c) Students who are disruptive should be asked to sit down. They should never be sent out of the room. Whatever further discipline is required should take place after class, in the office of the registrar or school supervisor. Children must always be disciplined individually and in private, never in groups.

d) Children who are ill should be excused from the class up to a reasonable point after which a doctor's certificate should be demanded to determine the cause of prolonged absenteeism. Children who are injured—a sprained ankle, for example—should be required to observe the class because they can learn from watching. In the first and second periods of study any child that is absent for one month, for whatever reason, should be suspended and required to start the period over when it is feasible.

e) It is a general practice in the United States for students to applaud the teacher at the end of the lesson. At Dance Theatre of Harlem this is discouraged. The class should finish in complete stillness. In intermediate and advanced classes the lesson ends with a *révérence*. In the ballet studio we are in a learning, not a performing, situation, therefore applause is unwarranted. Moreover, this applause usually degenerates into a meaningless routine that is devoid of sincerity or spontaneity.

Although the above are the basic rules for social behavior, the individual organization will undoubtedly find that others have to be added which are dictated by its particular environment. In large urban areas we are faced with the fact that groups of children living or going to school within only a few blocks of each other do not necessarily speak the same language. Each group develops its own idioms and creates its own symbols. It is no longer a question of racial or religious background, but something much more complex. In the ballet school we get a handful each of youngsters from these different life-styles. One of our first tasks as teachers is to help them get to know, accept, and understand each other. Once they realize that they are working toward a common goal, the barriers are broken down and something of social importance has been achieved.

As teachers it is imperative we bear in mind the fact that dancers are human beings first and after that dancers. Art emanates from humanity, and it is the teacher's duty to bring both of these elements into the classroom. Routine is deadly and untempered dogma is poison. Out of the millions of youngsters studying dance only a handful will ever reach a professional career, but what they have learned and achieved will be of great value to them throughout their lives.

In teaching dance we are concerned with the total human being; the physical, mental, spiritual and emotional make-up of the student are all involved. The development of physical prowess is only one small aspect of the complete picture. With dance, the student learns to listen, quietly and calmly, and respond to what has been said. Powers of concentration are strengthened. Observation becomes acute. Reflexes are sharpened. The result of this is that the youngster will make marked improvement in academic work, will read better, and possesses generally superior coordination. At a more significant level the young dancer becomes increasingly aware of the wonders of the human body, which is his instrument. This instrument must be respected and cared for, nourished properly and kept in prime condition. The misuse of drugs is taboo. Dancers are high on what they are doing and have little need of other stimuli. This can help solve a serious contemporary social problem.

Each student, regardless of apparent ability or lack thereof, has the right to be given attention. Without sacrificing truthfulness, the teacher should be encouraging at all times and no student should ever be demoralized. It is possible to maintain perfect discipline and ensure steady progress without undue strictness, cruel criticism or, worst of all, sarcasm. The student's confidence has to be won and kept.

If a teacher becomes bored with what he or she is doing, the fact must be faced and a decision made either to get out of the slump or stop teaching. The teacher, like all other artists, is a public servant. It is as simple as that, but for many it is too hard to accept.

✂ III ✂

Demonstration, Explanation and Correction

M ANY YOUNG TEACHERS, and quite a few older ones, are frequently dismayed by the fact that, although they demonstrate, the student doesn't get the movement; although they explain, the student doesn't comprehend; although they correct, there is no response. Often enough the pupil is blamed for being stupid or recalcitrant, which usually is not the case. Generally, the fault lies in the way the teacher has demonstrated, explained or corrected.

Demonstration is one of the most mishandled aspects of teaching ballet. It goes without saying that students must have a physical model to follow, but not one that dismays or distracts them. Young teachers, who are in their prime, are inclined to over-demonstrate, even dance the class along with the students. Sometimes, this can provide inspiration and incentive but, as a regular practice, it is detrimental, because, invariably, the student will absorb the teacher's particular mannerisms rather than the proper execution of the movements involved. In no case should the teacher ever use the classroom as a showcase for his or her technical prowess; such behavior is an ego trip that is antithetical to good instruction.

Extreme care has to be taken with demonstration, especially at the earlier levels of training, because children are instinctive mimics and will pick up imperfections like the most absorbent of paper towels. For example, if the teacher demonstrates *battement tendu* with a sickled foot, the student will follow suit and sickle his foot. If the teacher's foot is sickled by nature, this must be candidly explained. It stands to reason that we cannot correct imperfections in others if we are not acutely aware of our own shortcomings.

Each exercise or combination should be shown clearly, exactly and counted out precisely one, or if necessary, two times—but not more. The student must realize the need for total concentration on the demonstration and develop the ability to pick up what is being shown very quickly. If, during the students' execution of the exercise, an inordinate number of mistakes is made, the teacher must break it down, give one more demonstration, and the students should then repeat it. If mistakes are still made the exercise should be abandoned and returned to in the next class.

On any level of training, but particularly in the early years, demonstration has to be accompanied by exact and concise explanation. It is not enough to say: "Point your toes!" Which toes? How? Where? It is not enough to say: "Keep your fingers and your palm round!" Which fingers? What palm? What is round? All explanations have to be worded with scrupulous exactness; there must never be any room for doubt and everything should be reduced to the barest essentials. Economy has to be exercised to the utmost degree and metaphors avoided at all costs. It is easy to say to the young student: "Round your arms and pretend that you are holding a big beach ball!" But the student is not holding such a ball, and perhaps has never held one. The arms are being held in a particular and definitive position. The metaphor is built in to that position—no further descriptive embellishment is needed. We are intrinsically involved with the truth and depth of physical gesture and aiming for its perfection and purification—not with pseudo-poetic fantasy.

When we enter the area of correction we come into a danger zone and must proceed with caution. Without question an entire book could be written on the subject, but let it rest here with some rough ground rules.

It is not easy, because of our conditioning, but, whenever possible, the teacher should try to correct positively rather than negatively. For example, he should try to say: "Do it this way," rather than, "Don't do that!" The word "difficult" should be dropped from the teacher's vocabulary, and certainly never used on the introduction of a new movement.

Before making any correction, the teacher must be certain that it is the right one. In the analysis of a fault a keenness and quickness of perception has to be exercised that gets to the heart of the matter. Again precise observations and words are the order of the day. For example, if, in a jumping exercise, the student's knees remain bent, the teacher must find out why they are bent before saying: "Straighten your knees in the air!" As is often the case, the fault may not be in the knees at all, but, rather, in how the back is being held or how the feet are being used. Faults prevalently take place at a point higher in the body than where they reveal themselves. This point must be found before the right correction can be made.

Many teachers, possibly enamored with the sound of their voice and display of wisdom, correct without respite. They talk so much, there is little physical action in the class. This is a grave mistake as, more often than not, their words are lost on the wind and the students are frightfully bored. It is better to correct with action than with words. The students should be asked to repeat the incorrect action and then compare it with the right one. In this way their comprehension will be broadened.

If the same correction has to be repeated over and over the teacher is obliged to make an assessment: does the student lack adequate powers of understanding or has the correction been poorly worded and, therefore, unclear?

There are students who make deliberate mistakes to get the teacher's attention. This is a form of self-indulgence that must be recognized and discouraged. Students should be made aware of the fact that a correction given to one applies to all. When a class is divided into groups, those not actively working should observe and analyze what the working group is doing; this develops a sense of constructive criticism which they can apply to themselves. If the demonstration has been exact and the explanation succinct, the need for correction will be markedly reduced.

The teacher must correct, yes, but judiciously and with economy, because economy is the secret of what technique is about. Any excess is bad technique. The goal is elimination rather than complication.

The good teacher always bears in mind that he or she is not a pedant, but a leader-guide. The teacher's function is to transmit knowledge and not display it on the lapel like a decoration. The purpose and aim of teaching is to instill the best qualities of the past into the bodies, minds, and souls of the present and future.

✃ IV ✄

Elementary Principles

CAREFUL ADHERENCE to the elementary principles of classical ballet is mandatory because they form the foundation upon which this discipline is based. Without daily practice of these fundamentals the entire study is rendered valueless. Unfortunately, it is in the exercise of these principles that many teachers are at their weakest, usually because they do not know or understand them sufficiently, and are therefore unable to enforce them. The result is that students, who may have studied eight years or even longer, arrive at a point where they have to start again from the beginning—if it is not too late. The frequency of this occurence is deplorable. It is also in this area that teachers are prone to develop, and put into practice, some of the wildest and weirdest theories. Quite simply, an ignoring of the elementary principles is the most unforgivable kind of malpractice.

The following applies to all levels no matter how elementary or how advanced.

SPACING

Whether exercising on the floor, at the *barre,* or in the center, students should be evenly placed with enough space around them to move freely. Each one should be given his or her individual place and each made aware that this location and spacing must be maintained. Dancers have to get used to keeping precise lines, circles, and so forth from the very beginning. This gets them accustomed, in the classroom, to what will later be required of them on stage. In center practice they can be placed in staggered lines so that the teacher can see each one without difficulty. When a class is divided into groups, those not working should stand at the sides of the studio.

PLACEMENT AND BASIC STANCE

The dancer should stand as tall as possible; neck held long, ears over the shoulders, eyes at a level gaze. The shoulders should be aligned over the hips which, in turn, are centered over the instep. This places the weight so that the heels rest lightly on the floor. The toes do not grip the floor. The body should be pulled up out of the groin through the abdomen without any protrusion of the rib cage. There should be no pinching or contraction of the buttocks. The student should have the feeling that the navel is touching the backbone; this flattens the stomach. This is the ancient placement of the body, discovered by Leonardo da Vinci, which brings it into perfect balance; and balance of any kind is merely a result of correct placement.

TURN-OUT

The subject of turn-out has always been a source of contention. How much? How little? Whether to force it or not? Polemics without end, and all to no avail, because the indisputable fact remains that, without turn-out, classical dance cannot exist. Turn-out, besides revealing the body in greater and more noble dimension, expands the dancer's range of motion, making it possible to move in all directions easily and swiftly. Those who do not have a natural turn-out, at least to a certain degree, should abandon any hope of making ballet a career.

The objective of turn-out, or *en dehors,* is to turn the knees outward to a much greater angle than is usually allowed by nature. But turn-out does not come from the knees, it is initiated in the hip sockets. When the hips are opened the knees and feet follow in a subsidiary action. Strange as it may seem, this is something that many teachers do not fully understand and the result is a commonly heard instruction which can have disastrous effects, that is: "Turn out your feet!"

The hip joint is a ball-and-socket joint capable of great freedom of rotation by itself, but it is connected to a network of ligaments and tendons which hold and support it, without which we would be unable to stand upright or walk. It is upon these that relative turn-out depends. If they are flexible there is no problem, if they are not there is nothing very much that anyone can do about it. Tendons and ligaments can be strengthened and rendered pliable; they are stretchable, but cannot be stretched beyond the point that nature dictates without injury. The dictionary definition of stretch is: "to extend without breaking."

PRACTICE AT THE *BARRE*

In the first months of training the basic exercises are done with the student facing the *barre*. The hands are placed on the *barre* directly in front of the shoulders with the fingers and thumbs on top of the *barre*. The thumbs should never grasp the *barre* by forming a ring with the fingers. The wrists and elbows are relaxed. The arms, from the elbow to the armpit, are held parallel to the torso and slightly away from it so that there is space under the armpits. The abdomen is pulled in and the chest is lifted without protrusion of the rib cage. The back is not swayed. The torso is held squarely in one piece and there is no twisting of the body in any direction. For the achievement of correct turn-out, all basic exercises, such as *battements tendus,* are done to position *à la seconde.* Movements *devant* and *derrière* are introduced later. Relative turn-out is insisted upon. This can be forced, if necessary, because all too often the students can do more than what it appears they can do. To accomplish this the teacher must, with care, physically manipulate the students legs and feet into the correct positions.

POSITIONS OF THE FEET

Pierre Beauchamps is credited with having introduced the five positions of the feet, which he based to a large extent on fencing positions, in 1700. Since most of these positions had been in use for a long time, it is more likely that he simply codified them and put them into formal practice based upon a strict adherence to the 180-degree turn-out of the hips, legs, and feet. Over the years, and most certainly in this century, the five classic positions have been modified and refined for reasons that are natural, aesthetic, and very understandable. These changes have come about principally because of the alteration of the dancer's body and the kind of shoes worn.

First and second positions remain unchanged, but third position, except in *danse de caractère,* is obsolete where classical ballet is concerned. Fourth and fifth positions (with the exception of fourth position *ouverte,* which is aligned with first position) are crossed toe to heel. There are still schools that adhere to the old practice of aligning the heel of one foot with the big toe joint of the other foot in these positions. Such practice represents an adherence to obsolescence or a resistance to the evolution of technical tradition. A little comparison of the physiques of yesterday's dancers and those of today will make this clear. Within recent memory dancers had short, stocky bodies and heavily muscled legs which made it impossible for them to place their legs in perfect fourth or fifth positions. The contemporary dancer with long, lithe, attenuated limbs can do this easily and must be required to do it. In practice first and second positions have to be sufficiently mastered before the student moves into fifth position. Fourth position, being the most difficult, is introduced when it seems feasible. It must be noted at this point that it is humanly impossible for most people to stand in fifth position with both knees straight; if they attempt to do so there will be a locking of the knees that is injurious. Both knees straighten when the action of a *temps* is begun.

SUPPORTING AND WORKING LEG

In first position the weight is evenly distributed on both feet. The moment the action of a *battement tendu,* for example, is started, the weight shifts to the supporting leg, leaving the working leg free to move. In the exercise of *battements tendus relevés* to *à la seconde,* during the raising and lowering of the heel the weight remains on the supporting leg; the hip will rise and fall with the action but this is of no importance. There must be no shifting of weight. The student has to be impressed with the fact that both legs are always active so that the standing leg is firmly held and turned out throughout each exercise.

MANNER OF HOLDING THE HANDS

Without any tension in the fingers, the third and fourth fingers are held together. The index finger and the little finger are slightly open. The tip of the thumb lightly touches the tip of the third finger. This rounds the fingers and the palm of the hand. If it looks awkward at first the teacher should not be discouraged because, with practice, the hands will gradually assume the correct position. This manner of holding the hands should be maintained, at least through the second period of training, for the *barre* exercises, but, in the course of each lesson the thumb and fingers should be opened to the position that will eventually be used in performance. Constant correction is required, and this position should be returned to, even in the most advanced classes, if the hands show signs of losing form.

POSITIONS OF THE ARMS

Vaganova introduced a practical and effective system when she modified the basic *port de bras* positions from the elaborate Cecchetti method, with the argument that there are only three fundamental placements, plus a preparatory position: all other *port de bras* are simply variations. In the English school Vaganova's first position is called "the gateway of the arms." This implies a passageway through which one goes to get from one place to another, and the position is very much employed for this purpose; but it is more than that, and Vaganova had good reason for establishing it as first position. It is where the arms are placed in most *pirouettes* and, if the first position is not firm and strongly held, turning becomes impossible.

Preparatory Position: The arms are held down and rounded with no angling of the elbows, free of the torso, with space under the armpits. The little fingers are held about three inches from the thighs. The middle fingers of the right and left hands are about three inches apart from one another.

First Position: Without disturbing the placement of the arms, they are raised to the height of the diaphragm. They are kept well rounded, with the elbows lower than the shoulders and the wrists slightly lower than the elbows. The fingertips of both hands remain at a distance of three inches.

Second Position: The arms are open to the side. The relationships of the shoulders, elbows, and wrists are maintained as described in first position. If the student can glance sideways, without moving the head, and see the hands, the arms are correctly placed. The most common fault in second position is the tendency to pull the arms too far back, causing the shoulder blades to pinch together. The teacher has to be always attentive to check that this doesn't happen, because pinching of the shoulder blades is not only incorrect, but can lead to a painful condition which is hard to cure.

Third Position: The arms are placed over the head, maintaining the shape of the preparatory and first positions. If the head is held straight and the eyes are raised, the student will be able to see the palms of the hands.

The arms are held by the tricep and the upper trapezius muscles and not by tension in the deltoids. The shoulders must be held down without any strain in the shoulder joints. Again this is important for reasons of health, as undue or prolonged strain in the shoulder joints can cause bursitis.

Every teacher, provided he or she can control any temptation to go into amateur medicine, should own a copy of *Gray's Anatomy* and give it some serious study. One does not have to be a great anatomist, nor even possess the ability to name every bone and muscle to teach ballet, but a thorough knowledge of how the joints, tendons, and muscles function is essential. Without it the teacher is severely handicapped and the well-being of the student endangered. The ability to recognize and be able to correct any abnormalities (spinal weakness, pronated knees, flat feet, dropped metatarsals, to name only a few) forms a large part of what we are about as teachers. Let me hasten to say, however, that I am not concerned here with conditions demanding serious therapy; these are out of the hands of those not thoroughly educated to handle them. The average ballet teacher should not attempt such work.

EXERCISES WITH ONE HAND ON THE *BARRE*

As soon as it is feasible, beginners should start doing some exercises facing away from the *barre* and with one hand on it for support. If all has gone according to schedule this should take place in the third or fourth month of training. It is not advisable to keep children facing the *barre* and a blank wall for extended stretches of time. They lose contact with the teacher, become detached or bored and the result is restlessness with its attendant misbehavior. On top of this we cannot begin to put the basic principles into true practice or make much advancement, until the students are able to execute the exercises with one hand on the *barre* and the all-essential *port de bras* can come into play.

When the students do begin holding the *barre* with one hand, the proper position of the free arm must be insisted upon. The *port de bras* preparation before each exercise has to be carefully and exactly executed because, with these basic movements, we prepare the foundation for the intricacies of all future *port de bras*. This preparation is done on the famous "one-two" count that is heard in every ballet school in the world. Quite simply, to begin an exercise, the students stand with the arms in preparatory position; raise them on count one to first position; open them on count two to second position and place one hand on the *barre,* leaving the other arm in a well-held second position.

The hand is placed on the *barre* with the fingers and thumb on top of the *barre*. This hand is slightly forward of the torso and the elbow is relaxed so that tension is not built up.

The placement and maintenance of the arm held in second position are of maximum importance and demand relentless attention and correction. Mastery of this position establishes a firmness and stability throughout the body. The general tendency is that, as the student begins to do the given exercise, concentration is centered on what the legs and feet are doing and energy goes out of the arm, allowing the elbows and wrists to droop. This is another instance in which the teacher must physically place the student's arm in the correct position.

Some teachers, wishing to avoid the painstaking work that it takes to get the students to hold the open arm in a strong second position, take a short cut and let them put the hand on the hip. This is most inadvisable because it is a short cut that will eventually lead to a very long and disagreeable detour.

At the finish of the exercise the hand is raised from the *barre* to second position and both arms are lowered to preparatory position. The student's face is turned slightly toward the center of the studio. At this point he should take a deep full breath and exhale slowly and quietly. After a moment of stillness he turns to do the exercise on the other side. When changing from side to side the student must always be directed to turn *toward* the *barre*.

Under no circumstance should a dancer ever be allowed to drop the hand off the *barre* in a slovenly manner. Each exercise has to have the well-defined beginning and finish that these *port de bras* provide.

Part Three:

The Practice

ᘒ I ᘓ

Structure of the Lesson

THE FIRST PERIOD

T H E   M A T E R I A L presented below should, ideally, be covered in nine months with two one-hour lessons per week.

These first lessons are divided into five distinct parts:

Floor Exercises
Practice at the *Barre*
Center Practice
Walking, Marching, Running, Skipping
Sautés

The lesson time alloted to parts one and four is gradually diminished as the class progresses, giving way to more *barre* exercise and the introduction of basic *allegro*.

FLOOR EXERCISES will be discussed in the first lesson.

The elementary sequence of PRACTICE AT THE *BARRE* is:

Demi-pliés
Demi-pliés in first and second positions facing the *barre*. The students should not go beyond these positions until they are executed correctly; then they can progress to *demi-pliés* in fifth position. The *pliés* should be done at a moderate tempo with care taken that the lowering and rising take the same amount of time. The action must be gradual, with no hesitation or stop at the extreme depth of the *plié*. Proper pull-up must be insisted upon, with the center of the body kept in alignment between the heels.

Battements tendus

a) with straight knees from first to second position
b) the same with a metatarsal *relevé*
c) the same with a full *relevé*
d) with a metatarsal flex
e) with a full flex
f) with *demi-plié* on the return to first position
g) with *demi-plié* in second position
h) with *dégagé* to second position
i) with *passé par terre* through first position

The *battement tendu passé par terre* is not given until the *battements tendus* have been done *en avant* and *en arrière* from first position.

In the execution of *battements tendus simples,* or any *tendu* for that matter, the foot is brushed across the floor starting with the heel, going through the instep and the ball of the foot to the full *pointe.* On no account should the foot be lifted and placed in the pointed position, nor should the fully stretched toes ever lose contact with the floor, except in *battements dégagés* and *jetés.* The knees must always be completely straight, with the extension of the leg coming out of the center of the body.

The importance of the *battements tendus* can not be strongly enough stressed because they *are* the technique. Everything in classical dance is founded upon them. Too many teachers slough over them in an eagerness to get to more "interesting" things. This is a practice that is extremely detrimental; without persistent attention to correctly executed *battements tendus,* the muscles and ligaments of the legs will never be brought up to do the work required of them. Meticulous study of the *battements tendus* is continued even into the most advanced professional levels. There is a general tendency to speed up the tempo for *battements* as the dancer progresses into some degree of technical proficiency, an ill-advised practice that leads to sloppy execution and eventual impairment of the technique.

Cambrés

Cambrés are done first to the side and later to the back. The backbend has to be approached carefully and, in the beginning, the teacher has to assist by supporting the student just below the shoulder blades. The *cambré* starts with a lift of the chest and not with a ginching up of the neck or throwing back of the head. The shoulders are held down and the backbend kept in the top of the back, never in the small of the back—the arch there will form naturally. The pelvis must be firmly held, with no movement or thrusting forward of the hips. The *cambré* is an all-important action that has to be achieved slowly and correctly or the spine will be weakened.

Relevés

It is best to start the study of *relevés* with the feet parallel and about one inch apart. This position has to be exact, not a little turned-in or a little turned-out. In the parallel position any rolling of the ankles will be detected immediately. The student rises to the ball of the foot with the weight centered on the second and third toes. From here we progress to *relevés* in the turned-out first and second positions.

There are four degrees of *relevé: pied à quart,* in which the heels are raised only slightly; *sur les demi-pointes,* in which the heels are raised until the weight is distributed on the full ball of the foot or feet; *pied à trois quarts,* or three-quarter point, in which the heels are raised as high as possible from the floor and weight rests on the second and third toes; *sur les pointes* or full point, with the weight on the tips of the toes, which is usually achieved only in toe shoes.

When all has gone well with the foregoing, new exercises at the *barre* can be added:

Grands pliés

The study of *grands pliés* begins in second position, then moves to first position. The same principles apply as for *demi-plié.* When the *grand plié* is done in first, fifth, and later fourth positions, the heels are kept on the floor as long as possible and then rise softly and only as high as is necessary for the individual. When the extreme depth of the *grand plié* has been reached, the ascent must start at once; there must be no hesitation or stop at this point. Furthermore, the rise has to continue gradually through the *demi-plié* without any hitch or stop. There must be no abrupt or uncontrolled drop of the body into the *grand plié* and no accent used to press into the rise from it. The heels must not rise from the floor more than *demi-pointe.*

Demi-ronds de jambe par terre

Position sur le cou-de-pied

Battements passés and retirés

The difference between two similar positions, *passé* and *retiré,* has to be demonstrated and explained. In the *battement passé* the toes of the fully stretched foot are placed in the crook of the knee; in the *battement retiré* the little toe is placed against the supporting leg just below the knee cap. The latter is the position assumed for *pirouettes*.

Grands battements jetés

These can be introduced at this time. In the early study of *grands battements jetés* special care has to be taken that the shoulders, hips and arms are firmly held and do not lift or twist in any direction. The rudimentary approach to this movement is *battement tendu*, lift the working leg to the height of the hip if possible, return to the *tendu* position and close to first position. *Grands battements jetés* done with one sweeping action of the leg cannot be allowed until the student's torso is under sufficient control.

The elementary sequence for CENTER PRACTICE is as follows:

Port de bras

Demi-pliés

Battements tendus

Walking, Marching, Running and Skipping at various tempi, and in different rhythms

Port de bras to finish the lesson

When the teacher sees fit, the walking, marching, running and skipping begins to be replaced with jumps and basic turns:

Sautés in first and second positions

Echappés sautés from first to second positions

Changements de pieds, when the fifth position is fairly secure.

Soubresaut, when the fifth is secure

Pas de bourrée with change of feet

Basic *soutenu* **turns**

All of the above is subject to the level of the ability of the class and the speed with which it progresses. The teacher has to use discretion in following a logical pattern of development. During this first period of study the muscles and ligaments are toned and strengthened, the legs are turned out, the legs and feet stretched and the pull-up begins to be achieved. We are still at the stage of "rough, schematic forms" but the basic foundations should have been laid by the conclusion of the period. The temptation to hurry, which usually arises at this point, must be suppressed.

໕ II ໖

The First Lessons

FLOOR EXERCISES

THE TEACHING OF DANCE is a constant struggle with nature and the imperfections of nature. Hardly a child arrives these days who is not in need of some kind of corrective exercises. There are swayed backs, lifted or tilted coccyxes, round shoulders, or the now more common TV slump. Many youngsters have one shoulder higher than the other and overly developed muscles on one side of the back from carrying heavy loads of school books. There are pronated knees, flat feet and other foot deformities that come from wearing incorrect shoes. The teacher must be acutely aware of these problems and be ready to correct them with the proper exercises. Special caution must be exercised so that the student does not become hypersensitive or overly self-concious of his or her problem or great damage can be done. It is wise to correct with exercise.

To ensure swift progress the abdominal muscles must be strengthened and the muscles of the back strengthened and rendered supple. In the beginning a series of special exercises done on the floor is most effective. These exercises are not part of the traditional classic training. They are derived from the exercises done by athletes and gymnasts to serve the same purpose, and represent a valuable American addition to ballet education. They are eliminated when they have served their purpose. This moment of elimination will differ from class to class. Here the teacher must again use discretion. The following exercises are listed in the order in which they should be executed.

1. The student sits on the floor with a very straight back. The arms are stretched out to the side directly from the shoulders. The soles of the feet are placed together, the knees bent, the legs opening out to the sides. The student drops forward and grasps the ankles with both hands. The head is brought as close to the feet as possible. In this

position the student bounces gently 32 times. Then he sits up swiftly to the beginning position and repeats the exercise.

This simple but effective exercise is all too often misunderstood or poorly explained. The student does *not* bounce his head on his feet; the head should not initiate the action—the action is a gentle bouncing in the lower part of the back.

2. The student extends his legs front with fully pointed toes, stretching both arms out to the side directly from the shoulders. Then, bringing the arms forward, he grasps the ankles and bounces forward 32 times. He sits up straight with the arms outstretched to the sides holds this position a moment, and repeats the bounces. He finishes in a perfectly erect position with the back straight, the abdomen pulled up and the arms stretched overhead.

3. With his legs extended front, the student flexes up his feet and stretches forward, grasping the toes with his fingers. Again 32 bounces; sit up and repeat. If the student cannot reach the toes, he should reach toward them. He finishes with arms overhead as in exercise 2.

4. The student places his fingertips on the floor directly beside him with the arms straight. He flexes up the feet, then slowly points them, pressing through the ball of the foot to a full *pointe*. This action is repeated 8 to 16 times.

5. The student lies on his back with the legs together and outstretched directly forward, the toes fully pointed and the arms extended to the side with the palms on the floor. Alternating legs, he lifts one leg slowly up to waist height if possible, and lowers it in the same tempo. This is repeated 16 times.

6. Still lying on his back with the palms of the hands under the head, the student does 4 to 8 slow sit-ups. Often in the beginning either the teacher or another student will have to hold the student's feet to give the body leverage. Ideally, the student should keep the elbows well open to the side and the knees should not bend in the execution of these sit-ups.

There is a rest between these exercises in the early classes to allow for explanation and relaxation. As the student gains proficiency they follow each other in almost unbroken succession.

In the beginning these exercises should be kept in their simple, basic forms. It is unwise to complicate them in any way or the purpose of doing them will be lost. The only variations that are permissable are when the teacher is faced with a specific problem that needs special attention.

In the first lessons these exercises will take from fifteen to twenty minutes, but once they are fairly mastered the time allotted them should be reduced. After about six weeks they should be done in six minutes. Also, once the students understand what they are doing and to what purpose, they should be advised to do the exercises daily at home.

It is necessary to mention here that there is an exercise that is frequently and ill-advisedly employed by many teachers. In this exercise the student lies on his back and presses the small of the back into the floor. This is potentially dangerous and should be abandoned.

⚬ֿ III ⚬֯

Practice at the *Barre*

DEMI-PLIÉS
Face *barre* in first position

Demi-plié	1-2-3-4
Rise	1-2-3-4

Repeat 8 times in first, 8 times in second position (later in fifth position).

BATTEMENTS TENDUS
a) **Simple**
Face *barre* in first position

Tendu à la seconde	1-2-3-4
Hold	1-2-3-4
Close first position	1-2-3-4

Repeat 8 times right, 8 times left.
OR

Tendu à la seconde	1-2
Hold	3-4
Close first position	1-2
Hold	3-4

Repeat 8 times right, 8 times left. The "Holds" give student and teacher a chance to make corrections.

b) **Metatarsal** *Relevé*
Face *barre* in first position

Tendu à la seconde	1-2
Lower ball of foot to the floor	3-4
Raise to full *pointe*	1-2
Close first position	3-4

Repeat 4 times right, 4 times left.

c) **Full** *Relevé*
Face *barre* in first position

Tendu à la seconde	1-2
Roll down to second position	3-4
Raise to full *pointe*	1-2
Close first position	3-4

Repeat 4 times right, 4 times left.

d) **Metatarsal Flex**

Tendu à la seconde	1-2
Flex toes up	3-4
Return to full *pointe*	1-2
Close first position	3-4

Repeat 4 times right, 4 times left.

e) **Full Flex**

Tendu à la seconde	1-2
Flex foot up	3-4
Return to full *pointe*	1-2
Close first position	3-4

Repeat 4 times right, 4 times left.

f) *Demi-plié*, **first position**

Tendu à la seconde	1-2
Close first position	3-4
Demi-plié	1-2
Straighten legs	3-4

Repeat 8 times right, 8 times left.

g) *Demi-plié*, **second position**

Tendu à la seconde	1-2
Demi-plié, second position	3-4

Return to *tendu à la seconde* 1-2
Close first position   3-4
Repeat 8 times right, 8 times left.

When the above exercises have been mastered to a reasonable degree, the *battements tendus simples* and the *battements tendus demi-pliés,* first position may be done—still facing the *barre*—*devant* and *derrière.* If this looks all right, the teacher can introduce the next exercise.

---

h) *Passé par terre*

Preparation: *Tendu* back	1-2
Close first position	1-2
Tendu front	3-4
Close first position	1-2
Tendu back	3-4
Repeat 8 sets.	

CAMBRÉS

a) *Cambrés* (Side)

Face *barre* in first position, both hands on the *barre*

Bend to the right	1-2-3-4
Straighten up	5-6-7-8

Repeat to the left. Do the exercise 8 times in all.

b) *Cambrés* (Back)

Face *barre* in first position, both hands on the *barre*

Bend to the back	1-2-3-4
Straighten up	5-6-7-8

Repeat the exercise 4 times.

RELEVÉ (with straight knees)

Face *barre* in first position

Relevé	1-2
Hold	3-4
Descend	5-6
Hold	7-8
OR	
Relevé	1-2-3-4
Descend	5-6-7-8
OR	
Relevé	1-2
Descend	3-4

Repeat the exercise 8 times. The same exercise should then be done from second position.

Barre exercises to be introduced as soon as possible:

BATTEMENTS TENDUS

i) *Dégagé*

Face *barre* in first position

Tendu à la seconde	1
Hold	2
Lift leg sharply to 45 degrees	3
Hold	4
Lower to *à la seconde*	5
Hold	6
Close first position	7
Hold	8
OR	
Tendu à la seconde	1
Lift leg sharply to 45 degrees	2
Lower to *à la seconde*	3
Close first position	4
OR	
Tendu à la seconde	1

Lift leg sharply to 45 degrees 2
Hold   3-4-5-6
Tendu à la seconde   7
Close first position   8
OR
Lift leg sharply in second
   position to 45 degrees   1
Hold   2
Close first position   3
Hold   4

DEMI-RONDS DE JAMBE PAR TERRE

(If this exercise is introduced when the students are still facing the *barre* there has to be enough space between them and the wall to make its execution possible. If the *barre* is too close to the wall the exercise cannot be done until the student is working with one hand on the *barre*.)

Face *barre* in first position

Tendu front
Hold   2
Rond de jambe to *à la*
   seconde   3-4
Hold   5-6
Close first position   7-8
Tendu à la seconde   1
Hold   2
Rond de jambe to the back   3-4
Hold   5-6
Close first position   7-8

Repeat 4 times *en dehors*, 4 times *en dedans*.
OR
Face *barre* in first position
Tendu front   1
Hold   2
Rond de jambe to *à la*
   seconde   3
Hold   4
Rond de jambe to back   5
Hold   6
Close first position   7
Hold   8
Repeat 8 times *en dehors*, 8 times *en dedans*.

RONDS DE JAMBE PAR TERRE

a) **Half Circle**
Face *barre* in first position
Tendu front   1
Rond de jambe to *à la seconde* 2
Rond de jambe to back   3
Close first position   4
Repeat 8 times.
Repeat *en dedans*.
Note: Toe lightly touches the floor, gliding around smoothly.
OR
Tendu front   1
Rond de jambe to back   2
Hold   3
Close first position   4
Repeat 8 times.
Repeat *en dedans*.

❧ IV ❧

Center Practice

PORT DE BRAS

Stand in a comfortable first position to maintain balance.
Start, arms in preparatory position

Raise arms to first position	1-2
Hold	3-4
Lower arms to preparatory position	5-6
Hold	7-8

Repeat 8 times.

OR

Start, arms in preparatory position

Raise arms to first position	1-2
Hold	3-4
Lift arms to third position	5-6
Hold	7-8
Lower arms to first position	1-2
Hold	3-4
Lower arms to preparatory position	5-6
Hold	7-8

Repeat 8 times.

OR

Start, arms in preparatory position

Raise arms to first position	1-2
Hold	3-4
Open arms side to second position	5-6
Hold	7-8
Close arms to first position	1-2
Hold	3-4
Lower arms to preparatory position	5-6
Hold	7-8

Repeat 8 times.

OR

Start, arms preparatory position

Raise arms to first position	1-2
Open arms to second position	3-4
Hold	5-6
Lower arms to preparatory position	7-8

DEMI-PLIÉS, BATTEMENTS TENDUS

Repeat in center practice some of *barre* exercises.

WALKING, MARCHING, RUNNING, SKIPPING

These actions are done either *en diagonale* or in circles. They provide the possibility of some relief from the rigid disciplines of the *barre* exercises and familiarize the student with various rhythms and tempi. As soon as it is feasible, which is usually to-

ward the end of the first year or
period, they are eliminated and
replaced by the study of *allegro*
movements.

SAUTÉS

First position, arms in prepara-
    tory position
Demi-plié   1-2
Sauté   and
Land first position *demi-plié* 3
Straighten knees   4
Repeat 8 times first position, 8
    times second position.

❦ V ❧

The Second Period

THE MATERIAL PRESENTED BELOW should, ideally, be covered in nine months with two one-hour lessons per week.

The first month of study in the second year should be given over to review and consolidation of the first year's work. From then on, the lesson expands and takes a slightly different form from that of the preceding year. The Floor Exercises should now be done in five or six minutes. New movements are added to the *barre* work and the walking, marching, running and skipping are eliminated so that *allegro* steps can be taught.

1. The *ronds de jambe par terre en dehors* and *en dedans* are brought into full form. *Temps relevé*, which is the preparation for *ronds de jambe par terre* is introduced *en dehors* and *en dedans*.

2. The study of *battements frappés* is begun, first *pointé* and then struck. *Battements frappés* are among the most difficult movements to teach and to master so they must be given special and painstaking attention. This is one of the finest exercises for strengthening the toes and the instep but, more important, it is the basis for so many germinal *allegro* steps—*pas jeté*, for example. In the struck *frappés* the cushion of the middle toes is struck against the floor so that the foot ricochets to the height of about two inches from the floor. There is a particular sound to this, which is that of the striking of a rubber hammer. There should be no scuffing sound; if there is, the execution has been incorrect.

The placement of the foot for the start of *battements frappés* is open for discussion. There are those who favor the old Cecchetti placement which is with the heel either in front or behind the ankle and the foot fairly relaxed; then there is the newer placement which has the foot in a full *cou-de-pied* grasping the ankle. My personal experience has led me to believe the former is the best placement in the early grades, and the latter should be reserved for advanced students. The rhythmic execution of *frappés* is most important. The accent is always on the outward strike, where the foot is held firmly for a count or more; the return to the starting position is swift, unaccented and done on a half beat. *Battements frappés* can be contrasted with *ballonés* without a jump in which the accent is inward.

3. When the position *cou-de-pied* is mastered *pas de cheval* is introduced.

4. The next step is to *battements fondus,* another exercise of extreme importance. In *battements fondus* both legs must bend and straighten simultaneously with a smooth, non-stop flow of folding and releasing. In the basic *fondus* the toe is pointed to the floor.

5. The practice of *grands battements jetés* is accelerated and *développés* are introduced. When it seems feasible *arabesques* and *attitudes* are begun at the *barre,* along with *ronds de jambe en l'air.*

∽VI∾

The Floor Pattern

THE CENTER PRACTICE begins to alter at this time with the introduction of the positions of the body and the practice of *épaulement*. These positions, in which the dancer's body is turned at oblique angles to the front-center of the studio, are: *quatrième devant* and *derrière* also called *en face; à la seconde; croisé devant* and *derriére, éffacé devant* and *derrière, écarté devant* and *derrière,* and *épaulé.* To facilitate the teaching of these positions of the body a diagram of the floor pattern is used. In it the dancer is at point "X," and the spectator beyond point "1."

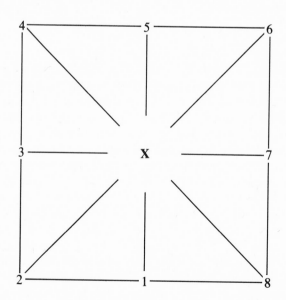

A sample of this floor plan about one yard square and constructed of canvas or linoleum should be employed so that the student can stand in the center of it and assume the required positions by using the corners or sides of the square for his focal points and not those of the room, which is usually rectangular.

Temps lié is a germinal combination of movements that rests in the center of classical technique and is the foundation upon which the entire science of *adagio* is grounded. It proceeds from its simplest forms, through endless variations, into the most complex phrases of action. With *temps lié* the body positions of *croisé* and *à la seconde,* with full *port de bras,* are amalgamated in a steady flow of unbroken actions which lay the basis for the effect of effortlessness that the finished dancer possesses. The teacher must spend a great deal of time and extreme care with this combination in the earliest grades. The entire body of the pupil—the torso, the arms, the legs and the head—must participate; any slovenliness of execution must be slowly eradicated, or both teacher and student will eventually be in for trouble. Once the student has mastered the simple *temps lié* a great deal of ground has been covered and the way is open for the variations that advance from *adagio* to *allegro.*

In the *allegro* section of the class the following jumps are introduced in the order given:

1) *Changement de pieds*
2) *Soubresaut*
3) *Assemblé*
4) *Glissade*
5) *Pas chassé*
6) *Sissone changé*
7) *Sissone simple*
8) *Pas emboîté* without turning
9) *Pas de basque*
10) *Pas jeté*
11) *Pas de chat*
12) If it seems possible, study of *tours chaînés en diagonale* can be started

Entrance into the study of *allegro* is an all-important step that must, of necessity, be made carefully and systematically. Any arbitrary progression in the study of jumps and turns can only lead to future damage or confusion. Any teacher who is undecided about this aspect of classical teaching should consult the sections on "Construction of Lesson" and "Jumps" in *Basic Principles of Classic Ballet.* No better description of what must be done, and how, has been written.

If the above seems overly ambitious, it is and it isn't. The above syllabus presents an optimum of material that the teacher must use with discretion. However, if the class is serious, this should all be accomplished, if in only schematic form, in the second period. Children at this point of development get very excited when they are learning new steps, which encourages them and spurs them on. All of these movements must be studied in their simplest forms; no combinations of them should yet be given. Combinations at this time are inadvisable because the student must be concerned exclusively and with full concentration with the proper execution of the basic *allegro* movements.

The teacher should consolidate everything that the students have learned at the end of the year, make sure that they know the terminology, and be secure in the knowledge that they understand what the movements are even though execution may still be imperfect.